DISCARD
WITHDRAWAL

✪ WEAPONS OF WAR
BATTLESHIPS
1900 TO TODAY

Smart Apple Media

© 2015 Smart Apple Media, an imprint of Black Rabbit Books
P.O. Box 3263, Mankato, Minnesota, 56002
www.blackrabbitbooks.com

Published by arrangement with Amber Books

Contributing authors: Chris Chant, Steve Crawford, Martin J. Dougherty,
Ian Hogg, Robert Jackson, Chris McNab, Michael Sharpe, Philip Trewhitt

Special thanks to series consultant Dr. Steve Potts

Photo credits: Art-Tech/Aerospace, Cody Images, Corbis, U.S. Department of Defense

Illustrations: © Art-Tech/Aerospace

Library of Congress Cataloging-in-Publication Data

Crawford, Steve, 1960-
Battleships : 1900 to today / Steve Crawford.
pages cm. — (Weapons of war)
ISBN 978-1-62588-041-3
1. Battleships — History. I. Title.
V815.C73 2015
623.825'2--dc23
                              2013032028

Printed in the United States at Corporate Graphics,
North Mankato, Minnesota
PO1649
2-2014

9 8 7 6 5 4 3 2 1

CONTENTS

Introduction

Capital ships

At the turn of the 20th century, the battleship was still king, but, by the 1940s, the aircraft carrier had changed that.

In any country's navy, the battleship and aircraft carrier are not just its biggest and most powerful vessels, they are also a symbol of that nation's maritime strength, its ambition, and its wealth. The ships described and illustrated in this book cover a huge variety of types and sizes of vessels, from early coastal defense ships to the vast nuclear-powered aircraft carriers of today's navies.

All the ships included in this book were all built to fight. That is their ultimate purpose, and the technical innovations which have attempted to give one ship a fighting edge over another has always been the driving force behind their design and construction. What began in the 1850s with steam engines in the hulls of wooden three-deckers, such as the French *Bretagne*,

MINAS GERAIS: see page 52-53

created within 40 years the big-gun battleship, epitomized by Japan's armored giant *Yamato* of World War II; the main gun turrets of which would weigh more than the entire weight of *Bretagne*. Ships such as the *Yamato* are the archetypal "big" warship, but smaller vessels of previous centuries are also classified as capital ships. The definition of a battleship is a large, heavily armed armored vessel armed with large-caliber guns. Thus, the *Ark Royal* of 400 years ago was one of the United Kingdom's battleships, just as the *Stonewall* was for the Confederacy 200 years later during the Civil War. The logical progression of this development is quite clear in the history of many of the ships featured in this book.

The *Agincourt* (1862), for example, had its guns set in a broadside exactly the same as the *Ark Royal* of 300 years before. It had a steam engine, but still relied on its sails at sea for economical wind power. Its armor was made up of iron plates backed with wood, making it literally an "ironclad". Like many of its time, however, it was already being fitted with rifled, breech-loading guns, which were more accurate and had a longer range than the old smoothbore muzzle-loading weapons. Its guns would also be firing explosive shells.

As guns were becoming more effective and munitions more destructive, the answer to that threat lay in more defensive armor. The French *Gloire* (1859) boasted a wide

DREADNOUGHT: see page 35

AGINCOURT: see pages 26–27

IRON DUKE: see page 49

WARSPITE: see page 57

Launched in 1860, the British Navy's *Warrior* was the first warship to have an iron hull.

wrought iron belt running from below the waterline to its upper deck, backed by up to 25.6 inches (650 mm) of wooden hull. However, wood was becoming obsolete. *Warrior*, launched the following year for the British Navy, was the first ship to have an iron hull. It carried four 70-pounder and ten 110-pounder guns, which outclassed *Gloire* and made *Warrior* the most powerful warship in the world. But not for long.

A British Navy officer, Cowper Coles, claimed he could disable and capture *Warrior* in an hour using a ship of his own design which cost half as much as *Warrior* to build, and which employed half the men. His secret was the gun turret. The *Prince Albert* was launched in 1864 and proved the potential of the gun turret, which could after all bring guns to bear on a target far faster

than any ship with guns ranged along the hull. However, it could never match *Warrior* as a sea-going vessel, being too lightly rigged with sail, and its steam engine was not powerful enough for the weight of the armored hull and the armored turrets, each of which weighed 111 tons (112 tonnes) and had to be worked by hand.

Refusing to be discouraged, Cowper Coles went on to try and prove the viability of a sea-going turreted warship when he built *Captain* in 1869. It was fully rigged and, to prevent the masts getting in the way, the turrets were placed very low to the water. Unfortunately all this made it unseaworthy, and it capsized in a storm during its trials, taking most of the crew and Cowper Coles with it.

THE TRIUMPH OF TURRETED WARSHIPS

By the early 1870s, armored warships with turrets had proved themselves in combat. During the Civil War in 1862, US Navy's *Monitor* had beaten the Confederate warship *Virginia* in the first gun duel between completely armored steam-driven vessels. But the combat was in shallow coastal waters and *Monitor* was later to suffer the same fate as *Captain*; on the open sea it foundered in heavy weather. It seemed as if such designs would always be restricted to coastal defense and shallow waters.

The drawbacks to armor and steam, however, did not curb the ambitions of either designers, ship builders or navies. It was clear that the advantages of a fighting ship with steam power, armor plate, and big guns were too great to be ignored for the sake of the practical problems involved in getting the right balance of all three. A ship needed enough armor to defend itself against the guns of an enemy vessel, a hull big enough to house the engines necessary to propel that weight at sufficient speed, and guns big enough to match, if not outrange, any others. It was a technical conundrum which the greatest technical minds of the age tried to solve, and which resulted in the 1870s and 1880s in huge variety of ship designs.

The position of guns in these vessels posed a special problem, particularly until the mid-1870s, when guns and turrets had to be positioned around the full rig of sails and masts most capital ships still carried. The guns needed to be sufficiently protected, but had to be high enough off the waterline to avoid being flooded and taking the ship down. Some vessels, such as the Turkish *Lufi Djelil*, had hinged bulwarks that could be

GRAF SPEE: see page 45

WEAPONS OF WAR

HOOD: see page 47

lowered to allow their turrets clear fields of fire, while others, such as France's *Caimen*, had guns placed in raised armored redoubts called barbettes. Another solution, seen in France's massive battleship *Dévastation*, was to have the main armament amidships inside a central battery.

THE RAM BOW

One feature, however, which characterized most ocean-going capital ships of the period was the ram bow. Designers were greatly influenced by the ramming and sinking of the Italian battleship *Re d'Italia* at the Battle of Lissa in 1866. Despite the fact that the biggest naval guns now had a range of over 15 nm (27 km), many saw the fate of the *Re d'Italia* as proof that ramming was a viable naval tactic and a practical use for an iron hull. For the next 30 years, warships would feature the chisel-like ram bow, and some, such as the Confederate commerce raider *Stonewall*, would be built specifically as rams.

However, this period of experimental warship design could not go on indefinitely. A fleet could not be sent to sea if its every vessel was of a different type, with different sailing characteristics, carrying a different caliber gun. In 1889, the British called a

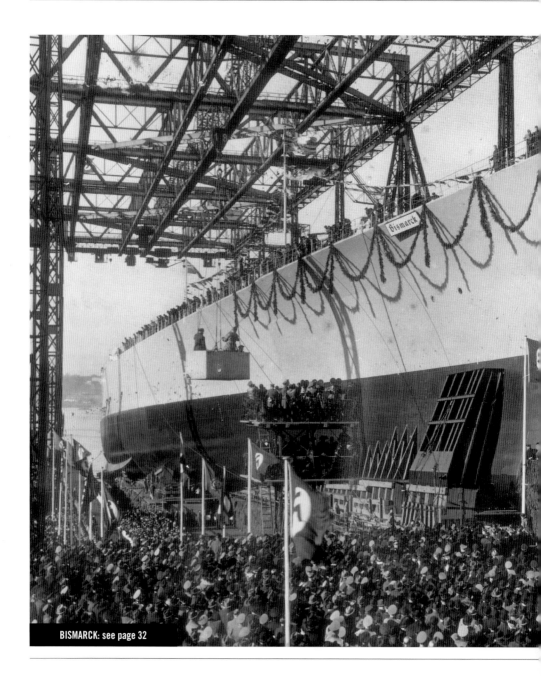

BISMARCK: see page 32

WEAPONS OF WAR

halt and ordered the building of an entirely new fleet of 70 ships, including eight standard first-class battleships. The resulting capital class vessel of this fleet was the *Royal Sovereign* of 1892. Its hull and guns were of steel, it was protected by armor plate up to 17.7 inches (450 mm) thick and carried guns of 13.5 inch (343 mm) caliber. Even though it displaced nearly 15,744 tons (16,000 tonnes), it could still travel at 16 knots.

BIG-GUN BATTLESHIPS

The era of the big-gun battleships had arrived. But the economic cost was enormous. Naval expenditures in the United Kingdom rose by 290 percent during the 1890s and, by the end of the decade, the cost of each new battleship was approaching $2.5 million (1.5 million British pounds). Not that such considerations caused any slow-down in warship construction. The world had embarked on its first great arms race, and every industrialized country — and many, such as Brazil, who weren't — saw the possession of a navy, and particularly battleships, as a mark of their power and self-esteem. The competitive spirit in this race was particularly strong in the new world powers such as Germany and the United States, who both spent twice as much as the British on their navies in an effort to catch up.

But the British had begun this arms race, for all intents and purposes, and were not going to risk losing their naval supremacy. Quality was what was going to keep the British Navy ahead, even though official policy (known as the Two Power Standard) stated that they maintain a navy bigger than

RICHELIEU: see page 56

WEAPONS OF WAR

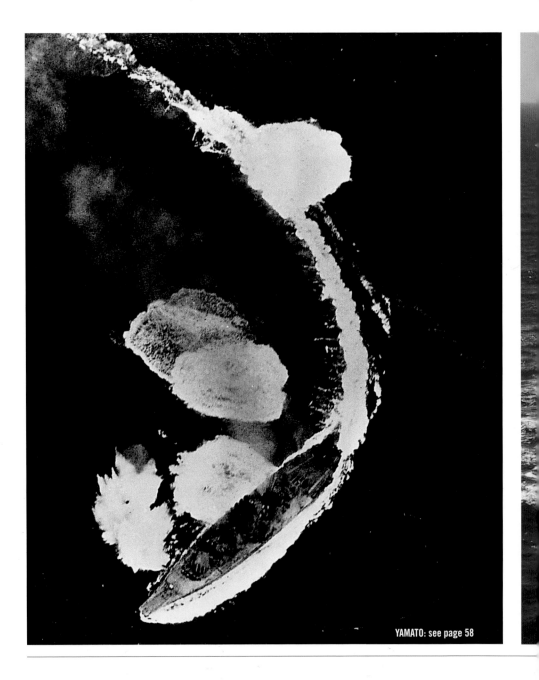

YAMATO: see page 58

WEAPONS OF WAR

IOWA: see page 48

any other two of the largest navies in the world combined. In 1906, they launched HMS *Dreadnought*, a ship which combined every single technical advance to date, from new steam turbine engines to electrically controlled gun turrets. *Dreadnought* made every other battleship in the world obsolete, including those in its own navy, and gave its name to an entirely new class of warship.

As with many of the record-breaking vessels of the past, however, *Dreadnought's* time as the world's number one did not last very long. By 1908 the British Navy was building so-called "superdreadnoughts", ships such as *Iron Duke*, which were over 8000 tons (8128 tonnes) heavier.

The future of the capital ship seemed to lie in bigger and bigger battleships carrying guns of ever-increasing size. But in the years just prior to World War I, questions were being asked about the battleship's future. While the sheer technical achievement in building them was celebrated, many — including senior British Navy officers — were wondering exactly how useful in battle these huge floating gun batteries would be. Countries such as Germany were ceding the battleship contest and were beginning to develop other warship types such as the battle cruiser, vessels designed for fast commerce raiding rather than naval battles, which would find ultimate expression in the great German raiders of World War II, such as *Scharnhorst* and *Bismarck*. More ominously, Germany was also investing in a fleet of torpedo-carrying submarines.

ARK ROYAL: see page 31

AKAGI: see page 28

WEAPONS OF WAR

ENTERPRISE: see page 39

ESSEX: see page 40

Aircraft were recognized as a potential weapon in naval warfare as far back as 1894.

THE FIRST AIRCRAFT CARRIERS

It was to be the aircraft, though, which would ultimately make the battleship redundant. Recognized as a potential weapon in naval warfare as far back as 1894, it was the United States who began work trying to fly an aircraft off a warship when, in January 1911, Lieutenant Theodore G. Ellyson landed a biplane on the converted deck of the cruiser *Pennsylvania*.

Aircraft were used for reconnaissance and target-spotting during World War I, but their offensive capabilities were not fully explored until the 1920s. Pioneers such as Brigadier-General "Billy" Mitchell in the United States proved that ships could be destroyed by bombardment from the air. In trials in 1921, his aircraft even sunk the ex-German dreadnought *Ostfriedland*, though it took two days of attacks and 19 bomb hits to complete the job. However, the United States Navy was convinced and, in 1922, its first aircraft carrier, *Langley*, was launched. Four years later, plans for

HERMES: see page 46

FOCH (R99): see page 41

Today, the US Navy's carrier battle group is the most potent expression of naval power in the world.

specially designed carrier-based aircraft were on the drawing board.

There was a new offensive weapon in the naval arsenal, but throughout the 1920s and 1930s traditionalists held firm that any future naval warfare would be decided by battleships, despite the fact that they were restricted by international disarmament treaties in 1921 and 1930, which effectively stopped battleship construction for 10 years and restricted gross tonnage when building started again.

At the beginning of World War II, battleships such as *Haruna* of Japan and the

British Navy's HMS *Nelson* still represented the most powerful war machines made by man. But by 1942, the type had been completely eclipsed by the practicalities of a new kind of warfare, and faith in the power of the battleship had vanished forever. Air raids by torpedo planes on Taranto and Pearl Harbor, the sinking of *Repulse* and *Prince of Wales* off Malaysia, the attacks on British battleships *Barham, Warspite, Queen Elizabeth,* and *Valiant* in the Mediterranean, all proved that a battleship could not exist without control of the air space above it. And while there were a few successes for the

GEORGE WASHINGTON: see page 44

old style gunnery warfare — the sinking of *Haruna* by USS *Washington* off Guadalcanal, for example — it was clear that the best practical use for a battleship was in shore bombardment or as a gun platform for scores of anti-aircraft guns. The age of the aircraft carrier as a capital ship had arrived.

CARRIER POWER TODAY

Since the end of World War II, the carrier has remained as the most powerful type of naval vessel, and the ultimate expression of national force projection. The US Navy's carrier battle group represents the apex of the aircraft carrier. A typical carrier battle group consists of one or two carriers, each capable of deploying aircraft (which on average contains nine squadrons of aircraft, including both fighter planes and helicopters). They are accompanied by substantial naval assets to protect them from both air and submarine attack: guided-missile cruisers, guided-missile destroyers, anti-submarine warfare destroyers, anti-submarine warfare frigates, and even one or two nuclear submarines; proof that the capital ship, no matter how powerful, is always vulnerable.

Admiral Graf Spee

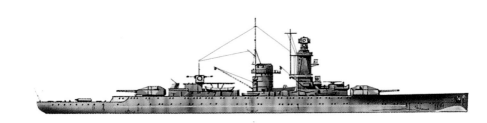

Limited by the 1919 Treaty of Versailles to a maximum displacement of 10,039 tons (10,200 tonnes), Germany produced the cleverly designed "pocket" battleship. Great savings were achieved by using electric welding and light alloys in the hull. *Admiral Graf Spee*, with its two sister ships, *Deutschland* and *Admiral Scheer*, were intended primarily as commerce-raiders. The ship was scuttled off Montevideo, Uruguay, after engaging three British cruisers: *Exeter, Ajax,* and *Achilles*, in the Battle of the River Plate in December, 1939. This ship was officially classified as being an "armored ship" by the Germans, though it was popularly referred to as being a "pocket" battleship, a title which stuck. In actual fact neither term is strictly correct, for it was in reality an armored cruiser of an exceptionally powerful type.

SPECIFICATIONS

COUNTRY OF ORIGIN: Germany
CREW: 926
WEIGHT: 10,000 tons (10,160 tonnes)
DIMENSIONS: 610 feet 3 inches x 67 feet 7 inches x 23 feet 7 inches (186 m x 20.6 m x 7.2 m)
RANGE: 20,000 nm (37,040 km) at 15 knots
ARMOR: 3 inches (76 mm) belt, 5.5–3 inches (140–76 mm) on turrets, 1.5 inches (38 mm) on deck
ARMAMENT: 6 x 11 inch (279 mm), 8 x 6 inch 150 mm) guns
POWERPLANT: eight sets of MAN diesels, two shafts
PERFORMANCE: 26 knots

Admiral Kuznetsov

The "Kiev" class could never be considered true aircraft carriers. From the 1960s onwards, the rapidly expanding Soviet Navy began to see its lack of such a vessel to be a handicap. In the early 1980s, two projects began to make serious progress, one of which became the *Admiral Kuznetsov*. Although superficially similar to American carriers, the Soviet aircraft carrier was always intended to be subordinate to missile submarines operating in their "bastions" in the Arctic. It is capable of engaging surface, subsurface, and airborne targets. The flight deck area is 158,235 ft² (14,700 m²) and aircraft take-off is assisted by a bow ski-jump angled at 12 degrees in lieu of steam catapults. The ship was designed to operate Su-27K, MiG-29K, and Yak-41 (and later the heavier and more capable Yak-43), supersonic STOVL fighters.

SPECIFICATIONS

COUNTRY OF ORIGIN: Russia
CREW: 2626, including 626 air personnel and 40 flag staff
WEIGHT: 45,864 tons (46,600 tonnes) standard; 58,462 tons (59,400 tonnes) fully loaded
DIMENSIONS: 999 feet x 219 feet 10 inches x 36 feet 1 inch (304.5 m x 67 m x 11 m) (hangar deck 600 feet/183m)
RANGE: 3850 nm (7130 km) at 32 knots
ARMOR: unknown
ARMAMENT: 12-cell VLS for P-700 Granit (SS-N-19 "Shipwreck") SSMs, 24 x eight-round Kinshal (SA-N-9 "Gauntlet") vertical SAM launchers with 192 missiles, 8 x combined gun/missile close air defense systems with 8 x twin 30 mm (Gatling guns and Klinok (SA-N-11 "Grison") missiles, 2 x RPK-5 (UDAV-1) ASW rocket systems with 60 rockets
POWERPLANT: steam turbines, eight turbo-pressurized boilers, four shafts, 200,000 hp (149,140 kW)
PERFORMANCE: 32 knots

Agincourt

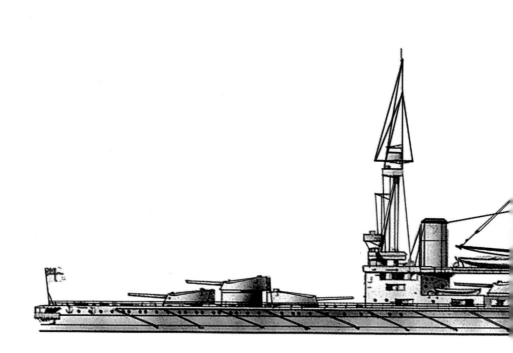

Originally ordered in the United Kingdom by the Brazilian Government and named *Rio de Janiero* when it launched in 1913, the Brazilians found they could not afford it. It was sold on to Turkey as *Sultan Osman I*, but never delivered. Completed in August 1914, it was appropriated by the UK Navy for war service and renamed *Agincourt*. In design it had many unusual features, not least its length and main armament of 14 12 inch (304 mm) guns on seven twin turrets. However, this huge amount of weight weakened its hull, which was in any case woefully underprotected. It was nevertheless known in its time as a good sea boat. Its tripod main mast was reduced to a pole in 1917 and later removed. After World War I, *Agincourt* was unsuccessfully offered for sale back to Brazil, and sold for scrap in the 1920s.

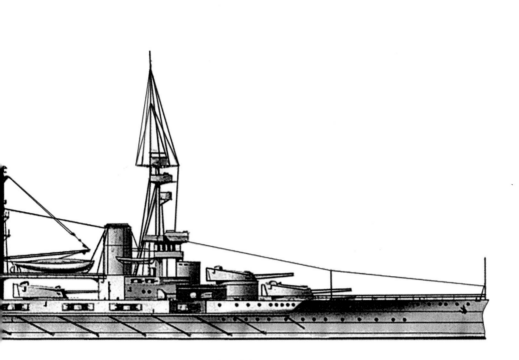

SPECIFICATIONS

COUNTRY OF ORIGIN: United Kingdom
CREW: 1270
WEIGHT: 27,500 tons (27,940 tonnes)
DIMENSIONS: 671 feet 6 inches x 89 feet x 27 feet
(204.7 m x 27.1 m x 8.2 m)
RANGE: 4500 nm (8100 km) at 12 knots
ARMOR: 9–4 inches (229–102 mm) belt, 6 inches
(152 mm) on bulkheads
ARMAMENT: 14 x 12 inch (304 mm), 20 x 6 inch
(152 mm), 10 x 3 inch (76 mm) guns
POWERPLANT: four-shaft geared turbines
PERFORMANCE: 22 knots

Akagi

Akagi was designed as a 41,161 ton (41,820 tonne) battlecruiser, but, while still on the stocks, the Washington Naval Treaty of 1922 (whereby Japan was forced to restrict its naval program) caused the design to be altered. Built to dispatch up to 60 aircraft, it was modified to carry heavier aircraft and more light guns. As converted, it had three flight decks forward, no island and two funnels on the starboard side, one pointing up, the other out and down. During reconstruction (1935–38) the two lower flight decks forward were removed and the top flight deck extended forward to the bow. An island was added on the port side. *Akagi* led the Japanese carrier assault on Pearl Harbor on December 7, 1941, but was destroyed seven months later by bombs dropped by US Navy dive-bombers at the decisive Battle of Midway.

SPECIFICATIONS

COUNTRY OF ORIGIN: Japan
CREW: 2000
WEIGHT: 29,114 tons (29,580 tonnes)
DIMENSIONS: 816 feet 11 inches x 100 feet 1 inch x 26 feet 7 inches (249 m x 30.5 m x 8.1 m)
RANGE: 8000 nm (14,800 km) at 14 knots
ARMOR: 6 inches (152 mm) belt
ARMAMENT: 10 x 8 inch (203 mm), 12 x 4.7 inch (119 mm) guns, 91 x aircraft
POWERPLANT: four-shaft turbines
PERFORMANCE: 32.5 knots

America

The Kitty Hawk class were the first aircraft carriers not to carry conventional guns. Intended to be larger and improved versions of the earlier Forrestal class, *Kitty Hawk* (CV 63) and *Constellation* (CV 64) were the first two built. The third, *America* (CV 66), was launched in 1964, and incorporated further improvements based on operational experience. Its dimensions are slightly different to those of its sisters, with a narrower smokestack. *America* was the first carrier to be equipped with an integrated Combat Information Center (CIC) and is also fitted with a bow-mounted sonar. A fourth ship, *John F. Kennedy* (CV 67), was built after the US Congress refused to sanction a nuclear-powered vessel in 1964. Policy has since changed, and all large US carriers since then have used nuclear propulsion.

SPECIFICATIONS

COUNTRY OF ORIGIN: United States
CREW: 3306, or 1379 with air group
WEIGHT: 79,813 tons (81,090 tonnes) fully loaded
DIMENSIONS: 1063 feet x 252 feet 7 inches x 35 feet 1 inch (324 m x 77 m x 10.7 m)
RANGE: 12,000 nm (21,600 km) at 12 knots
ARMOR: belt 2 inches (51 mm)
ARMAMENT: 3 x Mark 29 launchers for NATO Sea Sparrow SAMs, 3 x 20 mm Phalanx CIWS (Close-in Weapons System), 90 x aircraft
POWERPLANT: four-shaft geared turbines
PERFORMANCE: 33 knots

Arizona

Arizona, like its sister ship *Pennsylvania*, was an improved and enlarged version of the Nevada class, its main armament being housed in four triple turrets. Launched in 1915, and completed the following year, *Arizona* did not see any action during World War I. In 1941, it sailed to the Pacific to join the US fleet based at Pearl Harbor. On the morning of December 7, the Japanese launched an air attack without warning. One of the first ships hit was the *Arizona*. A bomb is believed to have struck one of its forward turrets, which detonated the magazine beneath. The ship blew up, taking over a thousand members of its crew with it. *Arizona* was one of four US battleships sunk at Pearl Harbor; a fifth was beached, and three more were damaged. Today its remains still lie in the shallow waters of the harbor where it is preserved as a war grave.

SPECIFICATIONS

COUNTRY OF ORIGIN: United States
CREW: 1117
WEIGHT: 32,567 tons (32,045 tonnes)
DIMENSIONS: 608 feet 3 inches x 97 feet 1 inch x 28 feet 10 inches (185.4 m x 29.6 m x 8.8 m)
RANGE: 8000 nm (14,400 km) at 10 knots
ARMOR: 13.5–8 inches (343–203 mm) belt, 18 inches–9 inches (450–229 mm) on turrets
ARMAMENT: 12 x 14 inch (356 mm), 22 x 5 inch (127 mm) guns
POWERPLANT: four-shaft geared turbines
PERFORMANCE: 21 knots

Ark Royal

Ark Royal was the first large purpose-built aircraft carrier to be constructed for the UK Navy, with a long flight deck some 60 feet (18 m) above the deep water load line. The aircraft carrier's full complement was 60 aircraft, although it never actually carried this many, as such a load would have reduced its fighting capability. During its war operations, *Ark Royal* took part in the Norwegian campaign of 1940 and was subsequently transferred to the Mediterranean Theatre, where it joined "Force H" at Gibraltar. In May 1941, one of its Swordfish aircraft torpedoed the German battleship *Bismarck*, destroying the warship's steering gear, an act that led to *Bismarck* being sunk some hours later by the British Fleet. In November 1941, *Ark Royal* was torpedoed by the German submarine U81 and capsized after 14 hours.

SPECIFICATIONS

COUNTRY OF ORIGIN: United Kingdom
CREW: 1580
WEIGHT: 27,720 tons (28,164 tonnes)
DIMENSIONS: 800 feet x 94 feet 9 inches x 27 feet 9 inches (243.8 m x 28.9 m x 8.5 m)
RANGE: 7620 nm (14,119 km) at 20 knots
ARMOR: 4.5 inches (114 mm) belt, 3 inches (76 mm) bulkheads
ARMAMENT: 16 x 4.5 inch (114 mm) guns, 60 x aircraft
POWERPLANT: triple-shaft geared turbines
PERFORMANCE: 31 knots

Bismarck

The 1919 Treaty of Versailles imposed tight restrictions on German naval developments. In spite of this, the Germans managed to carry out secret design studies and, when the Anglo-German Naval Treaty of 1935 came into force, were able to respond quickly. They began the construction of two battleships, *Bismark* and *Tirpitz*. As they had been unable to properly test new hull forms, they used the World War I *Baden* design. While they were equipped with powerful modern engines and were fine, well-armed warships, the dated armor configuration meant that the steering gear and much of the communications and control systems were poorly protected. In May 1941, *Bismark* was sent on a raiding mission into the Atlantic, but the UK Navy caught up with it. In the ensuing battles it sunk *Hood*, before suffering so much damage that its crew scuttled it.

SPECIFICATIONS

COUNTRY OF ORIGIN: Germany
CREW: 2039
WEIGHT: 50,153 tons (50,955 tonnes)
DIMENSIONS: 823 feet 6 inches x 118 feet 1 inch x 29 feet 6 inches (250 m x 36 m x 9 m)
RANGE: 8100 nm (15,000 km) at 18 knots
ARMOR: 12.5–10.5 inches (312–262 mm) belt, 14.5–7 inches (362–178 mm) main turrets
ARMAMENT: 8 x 15 inch (380 mm), 12 x 6 inch (152 mm) guns, six aircraft
POWERPLANT: three-shaft geared turbines
PERFORMANCE: 29 knots

Charles de Gaulle (CVN)

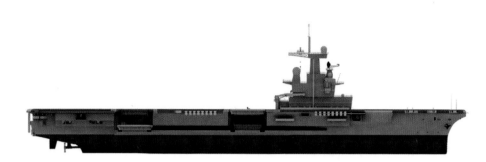

In September 1980, the French government approved the construction of two nuclear-powered aircraft carriers to replace its two conventionally powered "Clemenceau"-class carriers dating back to the 1950s. However, the French CVN program was troubled by political opposition and technical problems, both with the vessel and the aircraft. The first ship of the class, FS *Charles de Gaulle*, was laid down in April 1989 and launched in May 1994, but commissioned only in May 2001. The *Charles de Gaulle* is equipped with a hangar for 20–25 aircraft (around half the air group) and carries the same reactor units as the "Le Triomphant"-class SSBN, which permits five years of continuous steaming at 25 knots before refueling. It saw active service in Operation *Enduring Freedom* in 2001, flying missions against al-Qaeda targets. It had a 15-month refit in 2007–08 including new propellers, but required further repairs in 2009.

SPECIFICATIONS

COUNTRY OF ORIGIN: France
CREW: 1350; air wing 600
WEIGHT: 42,000 tons (42,672 tonnes)
DIMENSIONS: 858 feet x 211 feet 2 inches x 30 feet 10 inches (261.5 m x 64.36 m x 9.43 m)
RANGE: unlimited distance; 20 years
ARMOR: unknown
ARMAMENT: 4 x 8 cell SYLVER launchers carrying the MBDA Aster 15 surface-to-air missile; 2 x 6 cell Sadral launchers carrying Mistral short range: missiles; 8 x Giat 20F2 20 mm cannons; 40 x aircraft
POWERPLANT: 2 x K15 pressurized water reactors (PWR)
PERFORMANCE: 27 knots

C

Colossus

Colossus and its sister ship, *Hercules*, formed part of the rapid British naval expansion program of 1909. *Colossus* had an improvement over previous dreadnoughts in that it was built with stronger armor protection. To save weight, the aftermast was omitted, but the foremast — with its vital fire control center — was placed behind the first funnel, although this meant that it suffered severely from smoke interference. *Colossus* was one of the last British battleships to mount 12 inch (305 mm) guns; the next major group would carry the new 13.5 inch (343 mm) weapons. During the Battle of Jutland in 1916, where it was flagship of the Battle Fleet's 5th Division, it was hit by two shells. *Colossus* subsequently served as a cadet training ship before being sold for scrap and broken up at Alloa, Scotland, in 1922.

SPECIFICATIONS

COUNTRY OF ORIGIN: United Kingdom
CREW: 755
WEIGHT: 23,050 tons (23,419 tonnes)
DIMENSIONS: 544 feet 7 inches x 85 feet 4 inches x 28 feet 9 inches (166 m x 26 m x 9 m)
RANGE: 6680 nm (12,024 km) at 12 knots
ARMOR: 11–7 inches (279–178 mm) belt, 11–4 inches (279–102 mm) barbettes
ARMAMENT: 10 x 12 inch (305 mm) guns
POWERPLANT: four-shaft turbines
PERFORMANCE: 21 knots

Dreadnought

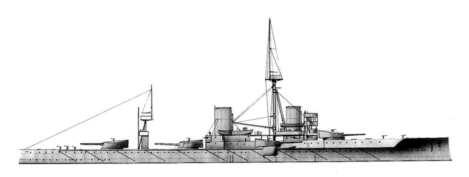

With the launch of *Dreadnought* in 1906, a new and more advanced era of warship construction began. *Dreadnought* was the first "all-big-gun" battleship, so much so that it made all existing battleships obsolete. *Dreadnought* saw active service in World War I, being surpassed only by even larger ships of its type, to which it gave its generic name. Despite its warlike reputation, during World War I it only sank one enemy vessel, a German submarine which it rammed. The UK Navy's Dreadnought fleet at the outbreak of World War I was thinly stretched, and after two months of hostilities, ships had to be sent to their home ports on the south coast for refit. This meant that two or three of the Grand Fleet's most important vessels were absent from active duty at any one time. *Dreadnought* was scrapped in 1923.

SPECIFICATIONS

COUNTRY OF ORIGIN: United Kingdom
CREW: 695-773
WEIGHT: 21,845 tons (22,194 tonnes)
DIMENSIONS: 526 feet 3 inches x 82 feet x 26 feet 3 inches (160.4 m x 25 m x 8 m)
RANGE: 6620 nm (11,916 km) at 10 knots
ARMOR: 8–11 inches (203–279 mm) belt, 11 inches (280 mm) on turrets
ARMAMENT: 10 x 12 inch (304 mm) guns
POWERPLANT: quadruple-screw turbines
PERFORMANCE: 21.6 knots

Dunkerque

Based on the British Nelson class battleships, *Dunkerque* was the first French warship to be laid down after the Washington Treaty of 1922. It was the culmination of a series of design studies that resulted in an answer to the German Deutschland class of the early 1930s. A hangar and a catapult were provided for the four scout planes which it was to carry. In October 1939, as flagship of the Brest-based Force L, it joined the UK Navy in the hunt for the German pocket battleship *Admiral Graf Spee*. It was employed on convoy escort duty until the surrender of France and, in July 1940, it was severely damaged by British warships at Mers-el-Kébir and by a torpedo attack three days later, with the loss of 210 lives. *Dunkerque* was scuttled in Toulon harbor in 1942, and raised and sold for scrap in 1953.

SPECIFICATIONS

COUNTRY OF ORIGIN: France
CREW: 1431
WEIGHT: 35,500 tons (36,068 tonnes)
DIMENSIONS: 703 feet 9 inches x 102 feet 3 inches x 28 feet 6 inches (214.5 m x 31 m x 8.6 m)
RANGE: 7500 nm (13,897 km) at 15 knots
ARMOR: 9.75–5.75 inches (243–143 mm) main belt, 13.25–6 inches (331–152 mm) on turrets
ARMAMENT: 16 x 5 inch (127 mm), 8 x 13 inch (330 mm) guns
POWERPLANT: quadruple-screw turbines
PERFORMANCE: 29.5 knots

Engadine (1967)

Engadine was laid down in August 1965 and was designed for the training of helicopter crews in deep-water operations. Although it did not carry its own aircraft, these could be embarked as necessary and housed in the large hangar aft of the funnel. At any one time, *Engadine* could carry four Wessex and two WASP helicopters, or two of the larger Sea Kings. Complement is 81, plus an additional 113 training crew. *Engadine* also operated pilotless target aircraft. It is a unique vessel, which gave a thorough training to the helicopter crews that formed a major part of the anti-submarine defense of surface ships. *Engadine* formed part of the UK's Royal Fleet Auxiliary (RFA), which consists of support vessels such as logistics ships, oilers, and tankers. It was fitted with Denny Brown stabilizers to provide greater ship control during helicopter operations.

SPECIFICATIONS

COUNTRY OF ORIGIN: United Kingdom
CREW: 75 plus 113 training crews
WEIGHT: 9000 tons (9144 tonnes)
DIMENSIONS: 424 feet 3 inches x 58 feet 5 inches x 22 feet (129.3 m x 17.8 m x 6.7 m)
RANGE: 5000 nm (9265 km) at 14 knots
ARMOR: none
ARMAMENT: ASW helicopters
POWERPLANT: single-screw diesel engines
PERFORMANCE: 16 knots

Enterprise (1938)

Early *Enterprise* designs had a flush deck, but this was thought to pose a smoke threat to landing aircraft, and an island structure to carry funnel uptakes and provide control centers was devised. The aircraft hangars were light structures independent from the hull, which could be closed off with rolling shutters.

Enterprise was refitted in 1942 after action at the Battle of Midway, during which its dive bombers helped sink three Japanese carriers. Apart from Midway, its World War II battle honors included Guadalcanal, the Eastern Solomons, the Gilbert Islands, Kwajalein, Eniwetok, the Truk raid, Hollandia, Saipan, the Battle of the Philippine Sea, Palau, Leyte, Luzon, Taiwan, the China coast, Iwo Jima, and Okinawa. It received five bomb hits and survived two attacks by kamikazes off Okinawa. It was sold in 1958, despite efforts to preserve it as a memorial.

SPECIFICATIONS

COUNTRY OF ORIGIN: United States
CREW: 2175
WEIGHT: 25,500 tons (25,908 tonnes)
DIMENSIONS: 809 feet 6 inches x 86 feet x 26 feet (246.7 m x 26.2 m x 7.9 m)
RANGE: 12,000 nm (21,600 km) at 12 knots
ARMOR: 4–2.5 inches (102–62.5 mm) belt, 1.5 inches (37.5 mm) armored deck 102 mm (4 inches) bulkheads
ARMAMENT: 8 x 5 inch (127 mm) guns
POWERPLANT: quadruple-screw turbines
PERFORMANCE: 37.5 knots

Enterprise (1961)

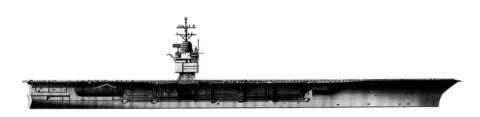

Nuclear-powered aircraft carriers had been suggested as far back as 1946, but cost delayed development of the project. *Enterprise* had a range of 347,581 nm (643,720 km) at 20 knots. When completed in 1961, it was the largest vessel in the world, and was the second nuclear-powered warship to enter service. Its stowage capacity was huge, including 2,720,000 gallons (12,240,000 litres) of aviation fuel and 2520 tons (2560 tonnes) of aviation ordnance. It was refitted between 1979 and 1982 and given a revised island structure. *Enterprise* carries offensive tactical nuclear ordnance that includes 10kT B61, 20kT B57, 100kT B61, 330kT B61, and 900kT air-delivered gravity bombs, 10kT depth bombs; 1.4mT B43 and 1.1mT strategic nuclear weapons can also be carried as required. Its air group is similar in size and configuration to that of the Nimitz-class carriers.

SPECIFICATIONS

COUNTRY OF ORIGIN: United States
CREW: 3325 crew, 1891 air group and 71 marines
WEIGHT: 89,600 tons (91,033 tonnes)
DIMENSIONS: 1100 feet x 252 feet x 36 feet (335.2 m x 76.8 m x 10.9 m)
RANGE: 643,720 km (400,000 nm) at 20 knots
ARMOR: classified
ARMAMENT: surface-to-air missiles, 90 aircraft
POWERPLANT: quadruple-screw geared turbines, steam supplied by 8 x nuclear reactors
PERFORMANCE: 32 knots

Essex

By the end of the 1930s, the increased needs of the navy for air cover led to an explosion in the size of aircraft carriers, and a larger hull was introduced to stow the aviation fuel required for the 91 aircraft now carried. There were 24 vessels in the Essex class, their designs based around an enlargement of the earlier Yorktown class carriers. *Essex* was laid down in April 1941 and entered service in 1942. It was removed from the effective list in 1969 and scrapped in 1973. *Essex's* battle honors in World War II included raids on Marcus and Wake Islands, the Gilbert Islands and Kwajalein (1943); raids on Truk and the Marianas, Saipan, Guam, Tinian, Palau and the Battle of the Philippine Sea (1944); raids on Luzon, the China coast, the Ryukus, Iwo Jima, Okinawa, and Japan (1945). In November 1944, *Essex* was damaged by a kamikaze hit at Leyte, and again in April 1945 off Okinawa.

SPECIFICATIONS

COUNTRY OF ORIGIN: United States
CREW: 2687
WEIGHT: 34,880 tons (35,438 tonnes)
DIMENSIONS: 871 feet 9 inches x 95 feet 10 inches x 27 feet 6 inches (265.7 m x 29.2 m x 8.3 m)
RANGE: 15,000 nm (27,000 km) at 12 knots
ARMOR: 4–2.5 inches (102–62.5 mm) belt and hangar deck
ARMAMENT: 12 x 5 inch (127 mm) guns, 91 x aircraft
POWERPLANT: quadruple-screw turbines
PERFORMANCE: 32.7 knots

Foch

Laid down in 1957 and completed in 1963, *Foch* is the second of the Clémenceau class carriers. It underwent a refit between 1981 and 1982 that enabled it to carry tactical nuclear weapons, and in 1984 received a satellite communications system. Further improvements included the introduction of a point-defense missile system in place of 3.9 inch (100 mm) guns, a new catapult mechanism, and a laser landing system for its flight deck. Its missile system was improved again in 1996. Despite these upgrades, *Foch* failed to retain a full air group. From 1975, it shared one with its sister *Clémenceau* and spent part of its time as a helicopter carrier. Its strike component consisted of the Super Etendard attack aircraft, which could be armed with AN52 15kT tactical nuclear bombs. It remained in service until 2003.

SPECIFICATIONS

COUNTRY OF ORIGIN: France
CREW: 1338 (as aircraft carrier), 984 (as helicopter carrier)
WEIGHT: 32,780 tons (32,255 tonnes)
DIMENSIONS: 869 feet 5 inches x 104 feet x 28 feet 3 inches (265 m x 31.7 m x 8.6 m)
RANGE: 7500 nm (13,500 km) at 12 knots
ARMOR: classified
ARMAMENT: 8 x 3.9 inch (100 mm) guns, Crotale and Sadral surface-to-air missile systems, 40 x aircraft
POWERPLANT: two shaft, geared steam turbines
PERFORMANCE: 32 knots

Furious

The origin of one of the best-known British aircraft carriers of World War II dates back to pre-1914 when Jack Fisher — then First Sea Lord — planned for a fleet of fast, powerful cruisers with shallow draught to operate in the Baltic. *Furious* was one of three such vessels built. Launched in 1916, it was converted to a carrier in 1917 to increase the Grand Fleet's aircraft support. Originally its flight deck and hangar were built over its forward gun positions. After undergoing a more complete rebuild, *Furious* served with the Home and Mediterranean fleets in World War II. Together with HMS *Eagle*, it was an invaluable asset in the early months of the Mediterranean war, flying off fighter aircraft to Malta. Its aircraft attacked *Tirpitz* in 1944 and it was taken out of operational service the same year. It was scrapped in 1948.

SPECIFICATIONS

COUNTRY OF ORIGIN: United Kingdom
CREW: 1218
WEIGHT: 22,400 tons (22,758 tonnes)
DIMENSIONS: 786 feet 4 inches x 90 feet x 24 feet (239.6 m x 27.4 m x 7.3 m)
RANGE: 3200 nm (5929 km) at 19 knots
ARMOR: 3 inches (75 mm) belt
ARMAMENT: 6 x 4 inch (102 mm) guns, 36 x aircraft
POWERPLANT: quadruple-screw turbines
PERFORMANCE: 30 knots

Fuso

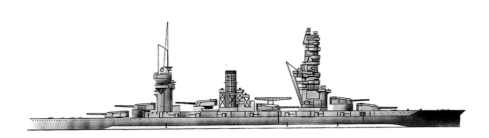

With the laying down of this vessel in March 1912 in a home yard, Japan confirmed its position as a leading naval power in the Pacific. Up until then, all Japanese battleships had been built in British yards. Although *Fuso* and its sister, *Yamarisho*, were less heavily armored than contemporary US battleships, they carried a heavier armament and were two knots faster. As originally completed in 1915, *Fuso* had two funnels, with the first between the bridge and third turret. In an extensive refit in the 1930s, this was removed and replaced by a massive bridge structure. Underwater protection was greatly improved and new machinery fitted. *Fuso* served in the Aleutians and at Leyte during World War II, and it was during the Battle of Leyte Gulf in October 1944, that it and *Yamashiro* were sunk by gunfire and torpedoes from US battleships.

SPECIFICATIONS

COUNTRY OF ORIGIN: Japan
CREW: 1193
WEIGHT: 35,900 tons (36,474 tonnes)
DIMENSIONS: 672 feet 6 inches x 94 feet 2 inches x 28 feet 3 inches (205 m x 28.7 m x 8.6 m)
RANGE: 8000 nm (14,400 km)
ARMOR: 12–4 inches (305–102 mm) belt, 12–4.7 inches (305–120 mm) on turrets, 8 inches (203 mm) on barbettes
ARMAMENT: 12 x 14 inch (356 mm), 16 x 6 inch (152 mm) guns
POWERPLANT: quadruple-screw turbines
PERFORMANCE: 23 knots

George Washington

George Washington is one of ten Nimitz class supercarriers built to date. It was laid down in August 1986, 17 years after *Nimitz*, the first of the class. *George Washington* carries extensive damage-control systems, including 2.5 inch (63 mm) thick armor over parts of the hull, plus box protection over the magazines and machinery spaces. Aviation equipment includes four lifts and four steam catapults, and over 2500 tons (2540 tonnes) of aviation ordnance. The life of the nuclear reactors is 15 years. *George Washington*'s air wing, like that of all Nimitz class carriers, comprises 90–95 aircraft, with two squadrons of Grumman F-14 Tomcats forming the interceptor element. The big carriers form the nucleus of a US fleet's Battle Force, the principal task force. Nimitz-class carriers and their associated warships have supported United Nations peacekeeping operations around the world.

SPECIFICATIONS

COUNTRY OF ORIGIN: United States
CREW: 5621 crew and air group
WEIGHT: 91,487 tons (92,950 tonnes)
DIMENSIONS: 1,092 feet 2 inches x 133 feet 10 inches x 37 feet 1 inch (332.9 m x 40.8 m x 11.3 m)
RANGE: unlimited
ARMOR: 2.5 inches (63 mm) on hull and magazines
ARMAMENT: 4 x Vulcan 20 mm guns plus three Sparrow surface-to-air missile launchers
POWERPLANT: quadruple-screw turbines, two water-cooled nuclear reactors
PERFORMANCE: 30 knots plus

Graf Spee

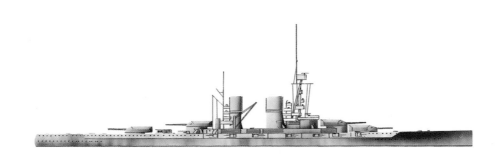

Graf Spee was to have been an improved version of the powerful Hindenburg battlecruiser launched in 1917. The main armament of *Graf Spee* was updated, the weapons being positioned in four twin turrets, two superfiring fore and aft. The secondary armament was concentrated on the upper deck in a long battery that was a continuation of the raised foredeck. The Germans hoped to complete all four vessels in the class by 1918, but although *Graf Spee* was launched in 1917, it was never completed and was scrapped in 1921–23. Other vessels in its class were the *Mackensen*, *Prinz Eitel Friedrich,* and *Furst Bismarck*; work on all of these was suspended in 1917 and the last two were never launched. By this time the German Fleet was virtually inactive — except in the Baltic — and materials intended for new-build warships were urgently needed in other sectors of the war industry.

SPECIFICATIONS

COUNTRY OF ORIGIN: Germany
CREW: 1186
WEIGHT: 36,000 tons (36,576 tonnes)
DIMENSIONS: 731 feet 8 inches x 99 feet 9 inches x 27 feet 7 inches (223 m x 30.4 m x 8.4 m)
RANGE: 8000 nm (14,400 km) at 10 knots
ARMOR: 11.8–4 inches (300–102 mm) belt and turrets
ARMAMENT: 12 x 5.9 inch (150 mm), 8 x 13.8 inch (350 mm) guns
POWERPLANT: quadruple-screw turbines
PERFORMANCE: 28 knots

Hermes (Viraat)

In 1943, designs were drawn up for a class of eight carriers, with machinery twice as powerful as that installed in the earlier Colossus class. Armor was to be improved, and a stronger flight deck was planned to handle the new, heavier aircraft then entering service. Eventually, only four ships were laid down, and the British decided to scrap these while they were still on the stocks at the end of World War II. However, due to the inability of many existing carriers to handle the new jet aircraft, construction was continued. After several design changes, *Hermes* was completed in 1959. During a scheduled refit in 1979, it was given a 12-degree ski ramp to operate the British Aerospace Sea Harrier FSR.1 V/STOL strike aircraft, to accommodate two squadrons of six. In 1982, it served as flagship during the Falklands War. It was put on reserve in 1984, and later sold to India and relaunched as the INS *Viraat*.

SPECIFICATIONS

COUNTRY OF ORIGIN: United Kingdom
CREW: 1830 and 270 air group
WEIGHT: 24,892 tons (25,290 tonnes)
DIMENSIONS: 737 feet x 100 feet x 27 feet (224.6 m x 30.4 m x 8.2 m)
RANGE: 4000 nm (7412 km) at 15 knots
ARMOR: 1.6 inches (40 mm) over magazines, 0.74 inches (19 mm) on flight deck
ARMAMENT: 32 x 1.6 inch (40 mm) guns
POWERPLANT: twin-screw turbines
PERFORMANCE: 29.5 knots

Hood

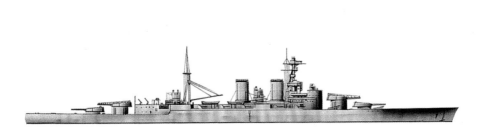

After the Battle of Jutland in 1916, in which three of Britain's battlecruisers blew up, designs were put in hand for a better-protected vessel. *Hood* was to have been the first of four such ships, but was the only one completed. Its engines developed 144,000 hp (147,381 kW), and range was 4104 nm (7600 km) at 10 knots. Despite being designed to avoid the fate of its predecessors, while engaging the German battleship *Bismarck* and the cruiser *Prinz Eugen* on May 21, 1941, its upper armor was breached by a shell which reached its magazine, blowing it in two. There were only three survivors, with 1338 were lost. The sinking of *Hood* was keenly felt by the British people, who held it in great affection. It had "shown the flag" for Britain several times, most notably in 1923, when it embarked on a world cruise. Its assailant, *Bismarck*, survived it by just three days before it too was sunk.

SPECIFICATIONS

COUNTRY OF ORIGIN: United Kingdom
CREW: 1477
WEIGHT: 45,200 tons (45,923 tonnes)
DIMENSIONS: 859 feet 7 inches x 104 feet x 28 feet 6 inches (262 m x 31.7 m x 8.7 m)
RANGE: 4000 nm (7200 km) at 10 knots
ARMOR: 12–5 inches (305–127 mm) belt and barbettes
ARMAMENT: 12 x 5.5 inch (140 mm), 8 x 15 inch (381 mm) guns
POWERPLANT: quadruple-screw turbines
PERFORMANCE: 32 knots

Iowa

Designs for the Iowa class of fast battleships were started in 1936 in response to rumors that the Japanese were laying down battleships of 46,000 tons (46,736 tonnes). *Iowa* was laid down in 1940 and commissioned in 1943. The class, including the *New Jersey* and *Missouri*, had greater displacement than the previous South Dakota class, and had more power and protection. The Iowa class served as escort for carriers in World War II, being the only battleships fast enough to keep up with carrier groups. *Iowa* was used to bombard shore positions during the Korean War. The last of the Iowas — *Kentucky* — was not launched until 1950. They were the fastest battleships ever built, with a high length to beam ratio; the armor belt was inside the hull. Two of the class, *Illinois* and *Kentucky*, were not completed. *Iowa* was damaged by gunfire from shore batteries on Mili Island in March 1944.

SPECIFICATIONS

COUNTRY OF ORIGIN: United States
CREW: 1921
WEIGHT: 55,710 tons (56,601 tonnes)
DIMENSIONS: 887 feet 2 inches x 108 feet 3 inches x 38 feet 1 inch (270.4 m x 33.5 m x 11.6 m)
RANGE: 15,000 nm (27,000 km) at 12 knots
ARMOR: 12.1–6.1 inches (302–152 mm) belt, 6 inches (152 mm) on deck, 19.7–11.6 inches (492–290 mm) on turrets
ARMAMENT: 9 x 16 inch (406 mm), 20 x 5 inch (127 mm) guns
POWERPLANT: quadruple-screw turbines
PERFORMANCE: 32.5 knots

Iron Duke

Launched in 1912, *Iron Duke* was the British flagship at the Battle of Jutland in 1916, and was one of the longest serving pre-World War I dreadnought battleships. It was a member of a class of four vessels that formed the third group of super-dreadnoughts. They were all armed with 13.5 inch (343 mm) guns, and were the first major capital ships to revert to 6 inch (152 mm) guns for anti-torpedo boat defense. Minor changes were later made to the secondary armament. The rest of its class was scrapped to comply with the Washington Treaty in the 1920s, but *Iron Duke* itself became a training ship in 1931, and was a depot ship at Scapa Flow between 1939–45. On October 17, 1939, it was attacked by four Junkers Ju88 dive-bombers of I/KG30 while at anchor in Scapa Flow and had to be beached after sustaining damage from near-misses. It was finally scrapped in 1946.

SPECIFICATIONS

COUNTRY OF ORIGIN: United Kingdom
CREW: 1022
WEIGHT: 30,380 tons (30,866 tonnes)
DIMENSIONS: 622 feet 9 inches x 90 feet x 29 feet 6 inches (189.8 m x 27.4 m x 9 m)
RANGE: 7780 nm (14,000 km) at 10 knots
ARMOR: 12–4 inches belt (304–102 mm), 9 inches (228 mm) middle belt, 2–6 inches (152–51 mm) on battery
ARMAMENT: 12 x 6 inch (152 mm), 10 x 13.5 inch (342 mm) guns
POWERPLANT: quadruple-screw turbines
PERFORMANCE: 21.6 knots

Iwo Jima

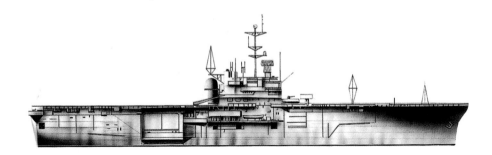

Iwo Jima — first of a class of seven — was the world's first ship designed to carry and operate helicopters. It can also carry a Marine battalion of 2000 troops, plus their artillery and support vehicles. The flight deck allows for the simultaneous take-off of up to seven helicopters, and *Iwo Jima* has hangar facilities for up to 20 helicopters. The two lifts are situated at the very edges of the deck, so as not to reduce the flight-deck area. Storage capacity is provided for 6500 gallons (1430 litres) of petrol for the vehicles, plus over 400,000 gallons (88,000 litres) for the helicopter force. In 1970, a Sea Sparrow missile launcher was installed, followed by a second three years later. *Iwo Jima* and its six sisters have extensive medical facilities, including operating theatres and a large hospital. Other vessels in the class are *Guadalcanal*, *Guam*, *Inchon*, *Okinawa*, *Tripoli*, and *New Orleans*.

SPECIFICATIONS

COUNTRY OF ORIGIN: United States
CREW: 667, plus 2000 troops
WEIGHT: 18,042 tons (18,330 tonnes)
DIMENSIONS: 602 feet 8 inches x 84 feet 4 inches x 26 feet 3 inches (183.6 m x 25.7 m x 8 m)
RANGE: 6000 nm (11,118 km) at 18 knots
ARMOR: 2 inches (100 mm) flight deck, 4 inches (200 mm) belt
ARMAMENT: 4 x 3 inch (76 mm) guns
POWERPLANT: single-screw turbines
PERFORMANCE: 23.5 knots

Jeanne D'Arc

Originally to be named *La Résolue*, this ship was authorized in 1957 as a training cruiser to replace the pre-World War I *Jeanne D'Arc*. Due to the cancellation of a large carrier, *La Résolue* underwent major design changes, emerging in 1964 as *Jeanne D'Arc*, a combination of cruiser, helicopter carrier, and assault ship. Its superstructure is situated forward, with the aft of the vessel being a helicopter deck below which is housed the narrow hangar. In its role as a troop carrier, *Jeanne D'Arc* can transport 700 men and eight large helicopters. In 1975, Exocet missiles were fitted, giving it a full anti-ship role. In peacetime it reverts to a training role, providing facilities for up to 198 cadets. The ship has a modular type action information and operations room with a computerized tactical data handling system, and a combined command and control center for amphibious warfare operations.

SPECIFICATIONS

COUNTRY OF ORIGIN: France
CREW: 627, plus 198 cadets
WEIGHT: 13,000 tons (13,208 tonnes)
DIMENSIONS: 590 feet 6 inches x 85 feet x 20 feet 4 inches (180 m x 25.9 m x 6.2 m)
RANGE: 6000 nm (10,800 km) at 12 knots
ARMOR: classified
ARMAMENT: 4 x 3.9 inch (100 mm) guns, Exocet missiles, 48 helicopters
POWERPLANT: twin-screw turbines
PERFORMANCE: 26.5 knots

Minas Gerais

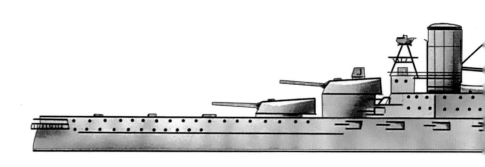

Minas Gerais was originally designed as a pre-dreadnought battleship in answer to the powerful vessels then being built for Chile. Its design was later modified and it became the first powerful dreadnought to be built for a minor navy. It was constructed in the United Kingdom and completed in 1910. It was extensively modernized in the US in 1923, and again in Brazil from 1934 to 1937. *Minas Gerais* was scrapped in 1954. Brazil offered the services of both ships of this class (the other being *Sao Paulo*) for service with the British Grand Fleet in 1917, after the country revoked its neutrality and seized German ships in Brazilian ports, but the offer was declined because of fuel problems. Tentative plans for Brazilian warships to serve in European waters in 1918 under the command of Adm Bonti did not materialize.

SPECIFICATIONS

COUNTRY OF ORIGIN: Brazil
CREW: 900
WEIGHT: 21,200 tons (21,540 tonnes)
DIMENSIONS: 544 feet x 83 feet x 27 feet 10 inches
(165.8 m x 25.3 m x 8.5 m)
RANGE: 10,000 nm (18,000 km) at 10 knots
ARMOR: 9 inches (229 mm) belt, 12–9 inches
(304–229 mm) on turrets

ARMAMENT: 12 x 12 inch (304 mm), 22 x 4.7 inch
(120 mm) guns
POWERPLANT: twin-screw, vertical triple
reciprocating engines
PERFORMANCE: 21 knots

Moskva

Moskva was the first helicopter carrier built for the Soviet Navy. It was laid down in 1962 and completed in 1967. It was designed to counter-act the growing threat from the US nuclear-powered missile submarines that first entered service in 1960, and to undertake search and destroy missions. However, by the time *Moskva* and *Leningrad* had been completed at the Nikolayev South shipyard, they were incapable of coping with both the numbers and capabilities of NATO submarines, so the building program was terminated. Classed by the Russians as PKR (Protivolodochnyy Kreyser, or anti-submarine cruiser) the ships proved to be poor sea boats in heavy weather. *Moskva* had a massive central block which dominated the vessel and housed the major weapons systems and a huge sonar array. It was scrapped in the late 1990s.

SPECIFICATIONS

COUNTRY OF ORIGIN: Soviet Union
CREW: 850
WEIGHT: 14,567 tons (14,800 tonnes)
DIMENSIONS: 626 feet 8 inches x 111 feet 6 inches x 25 feet (191 m x 34 m x 7.6 m)
RANGE: 4500 nm (8100 km) at 12 knots
ARMOR: 4 inches (102 mm) deck, 2 inches (51 mm) superstructure
ARMAMENT: 1 x twin SUW-N-1 launcher, 2 x twin SA-N-3 missile launchers, 1420 x helicopters
POWERPLANT: twin-screw turbines
PERFORMANCE: 30 knots

Queen Elizabeth (CVF)

Construction began in 2009 on a pair of large conventionally powered carriers for the UK Navy. HMS *Queen Elizabeth* is expected to enter service in 2016, with its sister *Prince of Wales* following in 2018. These vessels are to replace the existing Invincible class, and are vastly more capable. Displacing three times as much as the Invincibles, the Queen Elizabeth class is designed to operate an air group of 40 aircraft including the F-35 Joint Strike Fighter and Merlin helicopters. However, the vessels' planned 50-year service life is expected to far exceed that of the selected air assets. The design incorporates the capability of upgrade to accommodate future aircraft. This may necessitate the removal of the "ski jump" ramp at the front of the launch deck and its replacement with a catapult system. Defensive armament systems may also be added if budget funds become available. These will likely take the form of vertically launched Aster missiles.

SPECIFICATIONS

COUNTRY OF ORIGIN: United Kingdom
CREW: 600 (1450 capacity)
WEIGHT: 64,564 tons (65,600 tonnes) (full)
DIMENSIONS: 931 feet 9 inches x 128 feet x 36 feet 1 inch (284 m x 39 m x 11 m)
RANGE: 18,520 km (10,000 nautical miles)
ARMOR: unknown
ARMAMENT: 40 aircraft, including 36 F-35 Lightning II
POWERPLANT: 2 x Rolls-Royce Marine 48 hp (36 MW) MT30 gas turbine alternators, providing over 93.8 hp (70 MW); plus 4 x diesel engines providing 53.6 hp (40 MW)
PERFORMANCE: 25+ knots

Richelieu

Richelieu was first in a class of four battleships planned between 1935 and 1938, but it was the only one completed in time to see action during World War II. Launched in March 1940, *Richelieu* escaped the fall of France and joined the Allies in 1942, forming part of a powerful battle group that included battleships *Valiant*, *Howe,* and *Queen Elizabeth*; battlecruiser *Renown;* and carriers *Victorious*, *Illustrious,* and *Indomitable.* It escorted many attack sorties by the carriers on Java, Sumatra and the various enemy-held island groups in the Indian Ocean. *Richelieu* underwent a substantial refit in the USA in 1943, when radar and an extra 100 antiaircraft guns were added. Joining the British Eastern Fleet in 1944, it served until the end of the war. It later operated off Indo-China during France's war there. *Richelieu* was paid off and hulked in 1959, and was broken up in 1964.

SPECIFICATIONS

COUNTRY OF ORIGIN: France
CREW: 1670
WEIGHT: 47,8500 tons (47,000 tonnes)
DIMENSIONS: 813 feet 2 inches x 108 feet 3 inches x 32 feet 8 inches (247.85 m x 33 m x 9.63 m)
RANGE: 6000 nm (10,800 km) at 12 knots
ARMOR: 13.5–9.75 inches (342–243 mm) belt
ARMAMENT: 8 x 15 inch (380 mm), 9 x 6 inch (152 mm) guns
POWERPLANT: 4 x Parsons geared turbines; 6 x Indret Sural boilers
PERFORMANCE: 30 knots

Warspite

Completed in 1916, *Warspite* belonged to the Queen Elizabeth class, developed from the Iron Duke class, but its displacement was increased by 2500 tons (2540 tonnes), and 20 feet (6 m) were added to the length. The 15 inch (380 mm) guns fired an 1916 pound (871 kg) shell to a range of 20 miles (32 km) with extreme accuracy. It was badly damaged at Jutland, taking 15 hits from 11 inch (279 mm) 12 inch (304 mm) shells. *Warspite* was extensively modernized between 1934 and 1937. During operations in World War II, it was severely damaged by German bombs off Crete, and later by German radio-controlled bombs off Salerno, Italy, when covering the Allied landings. It was partially repaired, and used as part of the bombardment force covering the D-Day landings in Normandy. *Warspite* was further damaged by a mine off Harwich on June 13, 1944. It was paid off in 1945 and scrapped in 1948.

SPECIFICATIONS

COUNTRY OF ORIGIN: United Kingdom
CREW: 951
WEIGHT: 33,020 tons (33,548 tonnes)
DIMENSIONS: 646 feet 4 inches x 90 feet 6 inches x 29 feet 10 inches (197 m x 28 m x 9 m)
RANGE: 4500 nm (8100 km) at 10 knots
ARMOR: 13–6.6 inches (330–168 mm) belt, 13–5 inches (330–127 mm) on turrets, 10–4 inches (254–102 mm) on barbettes
ARMAMENT: 8 x 15 inch (380 mm), 16 x 6 inch (152 mm) guns
POWERPLANT: quadruple-screw turbines
PERFORMANCE: 23 knots

Yamato

Yamato, together with its sister *Musashi*, were the world's largest and most powerful battleships ever built when they were launched. No fewer than 23 designs were prepared for *Yamato* between 1934 and 1937 when it was laid down. When it was launched, its displacement was only surpassed by that of the British liner *Queen Mary*. Its main turrets each weighed 2774 tons (2818 tonnes), and each 18.1 inch (460 mm) gun could fire two 3240 pound (1473 kg) shells per minute over a distance of 25 miles (41 km). As flagship of the Combined Fleet, *Yamato* saw action in the battles of Midway, the Philippine Sea, and Leyte Gulf. On December 25, 1943, it was torpedoed by the US submarine *Skate* south of Truk, and in October 1944, it was damaged by two bomb hits at Leyte Gulf. On April 7, 1945, *Yamato* was sunk by US carrier aircraft 130 miles southwest of Kagoshima with the loss of 2498 lives.

SPECIFICATIONS

COUNTRY OF ORIGIN: Japan
CREW: 2500
WEIGHT: 71,659 tons (71,110 tonnes)
DIMENSIONS: 862 feet 10 inches x 121 feet 1 inch x 33 feet 10 inches (263 m x 36.9 m x 10.3 m)
RANGE: 7200 nm (13,340 km) at 16 knots
ARMOR: 16.1 inches (408 mm) belt, 9.1–7.9 inches (231–200 mm) deck, 21.5 inches (546 mm) on barbettes, 25.6–7.6 inches (650–193 mm) on main turrets
ARMAMENT: 9 x 18.1 inch (460 mm), 12 x 6.1 inch (155 mm), 12 x 5 inch (127 mm) guns
POWERPLANT: quadruple-screw turbines
PERFORMANCE: 27 knots

Zuikaku

Zuikaku and its sister, *Shokaku*, were the most successful carriers operated by the Japanese Navy. They were considerably larger than previous purpose-built carriers, and were better armed, better protected, and carried more aircraft. The wooden flight deck was 787 feet (240 m) long and 95 feet (29 m) wide, and was serviced by three lifts. *Zuikaku* formed part of the carrier task force whose aircraft attacked the US Pacific Fleet base at Pearl Harbor in December 1941, and subsequently participated in every notable fleet action of the Pacific war: Java, Ceylon, the Coral Sea, the Eastern Solomons, Santa Cruz, the Philippine Sea, and Leyte Gulf. Its name means Lucky Crane and its sister ship was *Shokaku* (Happy Crane), sunk in June 1944 by the US submarine *Cavalla*. *Zuikaku* was sunk in action by American forces on October 25, 1944, during the Battle of Cape Engano in Leyte Gulf.

SPECIFICATIONS

COUNTRY OF ORIGIN: Japan
CREW: 1660
WEIGHT: 32,105 tons (32,618 tonnes)
DIMENSIONS: 843 feet 2 inches x 95 feet 2 inches x 29 feet (257 m x 29 m x 8.8 m)
RANGE: 9700 nm (17,974 km) at 18 knots
ARMOR: 1.8 inches (45 mm) belt, 6.5 inches (162.5) over magazines, 3.9 inches (97.5 mm) on flight deck
ARMAMENT: 16 x 5 inch (127 mm) guns
POWERPLANT: quadruple-screw turbines
PERFORMANCE: 34.2 knots

BATTLESHIPS

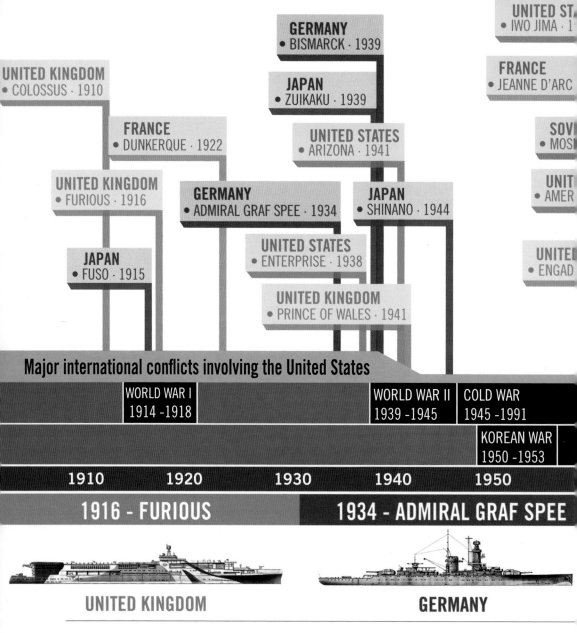

UNITED ST.
- IWO JIMA · 1

GERMANY
- BISMARCK · 1939

FRANCE
- JEANNE D'ARC

UNITED KINGDOM
- COLOSSUS · 1910

JAPAN
- ZUIKAKU · 1939

SOV
- MOS

FRANCE
- DUNKERQUE · 1922

UNITED STATES
- ARIZONA · 1941

UNITED KINGDOM
- FURIOUS · 1916

GERMANY
- ADMIRAL GRAF SPEE · 1934

JAPAN
- SHINANO · 1944

UNIT
- AMER

JAPAN
- FUSO · 1915

UNITED STATES
- ENTERPRISE · 1938

UNITED
- ENGAD

UNITED KINGDOM
- PRINCE OF WALES · 1941

Major international conflicts involving the United States

WORLD WAR I 1914 -1918		WORLD WAR II 1939 -1945	COLD WAR 1945 -1991
			KOREAN WAR 1950 -1953

1910	1920	1930	1940	1950

1916 - FURIOUS

1934 - ADMIRAL GRAF SPEE

UNITED KINGDOM

GERMANY

FEATURED WEAPONS TIMELINE

This timeline features notable advancements in military technologies by influential nations worldwide.

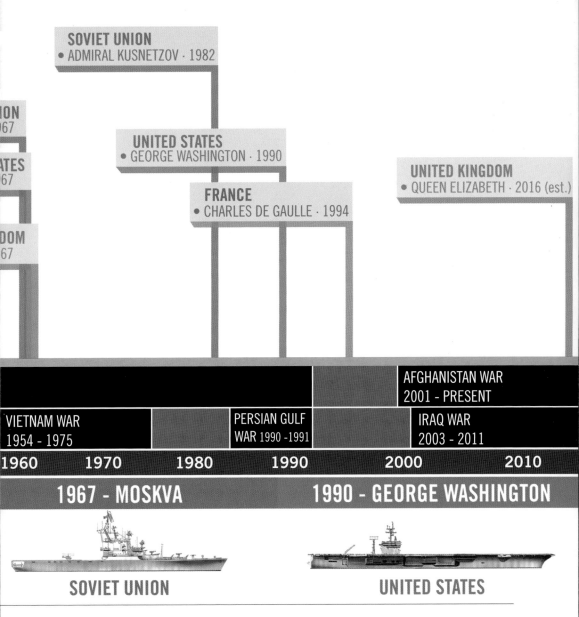

SOVIET UNION
- ADMIRAL KUSNETZOV · 1982

UNITED STATES
- GEORGE WASHINGTON · 1990

FRANCE
- CHARLES DE GAULLE · 1994

UNITED KINGDOM
- QUEEN ELIZABETH · 2016 (est.)

ION
67

ATES
67

DOM
67

	AFGHANISTAN WAR 2001 - PRESENT	
VIETNAM WAR 1954 - 1975	PERSIAN GULF WAR 1990 -1991	IRAQ WAR 2003 - 2011

1960	1970	1980	1990	2000	2010

1967 - MOSKVA   1990 - GEORGE WASHINGTON

SOVIET UNION   **UNITED STATES**

Glossary

archetypal
the original model; a perfect example

armament
the weapons and supplies of war that equips a
military unit

arms race
a competition between two or more nations to have
the best armed forces

arsenal
storage and accumulation of weapons
and ammunition

battery
the guns of a warship

breech-loading
loading ammunition in a chamber that is in the
rear portion of the barrel instead of the muzzle

broadside
the side of a vessel

bulwarks
a wall or similar structure that provides a defense
from an attack

capital ships
a warship of the largest and strongest class (battle
ship, aircraft carrier) and most heavily armed

ceding
to yield or grant usually by a treaty

commerce raiding
a form of naval warfare to attack or destroy the
merchant shipping of the enemy

conundrum
an intricate problem that cannot be solved

disarmament treaties
agreements to limit or stop the manufacture or
buying of weapons

frigates
A modern warship used for escort duty to protect
other warships that deliver troops and supplies.

gun batteries
the whole armament of a warship

gun turret
a covered platform mounted on the ship to protect
the crew and the mechanism of a weapon that can
be aimed and fired in many directions

hulls
the watertight body of a ship or boat

innovations
new ideas, devices, or methods

knot
a unit of speed equal to 1 nautical mile (1.85 km)
per hour, approximately 1.15 miles per hour

reconnaissance
the actions to gain information about the enemy
such as number of troops, weapons, and position

redoubts
structures or places to resist attack and defend an
approach by the enemy

smoothbore muzzle-loading weapons
a firearm in which the projectile and the propellant
charge are loaded from the end of a smooth barrel
and can be less accurate

turrets
a revolving domelike structure on a military tank,
plane, or ship with guns mounted on it

waterline
a line on the outside of a ship that matches the
surface of the water when the ship floats evenly
under specified conditions of loading weight

Further Information

Websites

http://usmilitary.about.com/library/milinfo/navyfacts/bldestroyers.htm
This site offers information on the background and features of a destroyer.

http://www.militaryfactory.com/armor/index.asp
This site presents information from the early destroyers to modern destroyers.

www.mvpa.org/
The Military Vehicle Preservation Association is an international organization dedicated to the collection and restoration of historic military vehicles.

www.mvtf.org/
See one of the largest collections of historical military vehicles, overseen by the Military Vehicle Technology Foundation.

Books

Cooke, Tim. *Warships.* Smart Apple Media, 2012.
A close-up look at the top military warships from around the world and their role in combat and defense.

Roberts, John. *The Battleship Dreadnought (Anatomy of the Ship).* Conway, 2013.
The legendary Dreadnought revolutionized the design of battleships.

Scarpi, Wayne. *Battleship Nevada the Extraordinary Ship of Firsts.* Nimble Books, 2008.
The Nevada is one of the most famous battleships to ever serve the US Navy in World War II.

Zimmerman, W. Frederick. *BB-67 Montana United States Battleship: Why She Matters Today.* Nimble Books, 2008.
Battleship Montana is the largest battleship ever planned by the US Navy.

Index of Battleships Profile Pages